How to Be
Happily Retired

by

Dr. Denis Waitley
and
Eudora Seyfer

CELESTIAL ARTS
Berkeley, California

ACKNOWLEDGEMENTS

This book combines the achievement and insights of Dr. Denis Waitley
(not retired) with the research and experiences of Eudora Seyfer (retired).

The authors gratefully acknowledge the contributions of the following individuals:
Liz Carpenter, President Jimmy Carter, First Lady Rosalynn Carter, Julia Child,
Norman Cousins, Carmen Dell'Orefice, Phyllis Diller, Harriet Doerr, Ken
Dychtwald, Betty Friedan, Connie Goldman, Lee Iacocca, Jack LaLanne, Angela
Lansbury, Madeleine L'Engle, James Michener, Wilfred Peterson, May Sarton,
Studs Terkel, and Peter Ustinov.

Library of Congress Cataloging-in-Publication Data:

Seyfer, Eudora, 1925–
    How to be happily retired / by Eudora Seyfer and Denis Waitley.
        p.   cm.
    Includes bibliographical references (p. 89).
    ISBN 0-89087-761-0
    1. Retirement—United States.   2. Retirement—United States—Planning.
I. Waitley, Denis.   II. Title.
HQ1062.S49   1995
646.7'9—dc20   95-33045
                                                              CIP

Celestial Arts Publishing
P.O. Box 7123
Berkeley, CA 94707

CONTENTS

INTRODUCTION

It is a fact: Purpose is the engine that powers our lives.

When people retire, often they unexpectedly find themselves without purpose. After years devoted to competing, acquiring, accumulating, and providing, life seems suddenly pointless. And when these new retirees look about for new goals and a new lifestyle, there seems to be nothing to replace the old. As a result, the wonderful, euphoric feelings of joy and freedom which most people feel when they first retire turn to bewilderment. What now? Is this all there is?

Sooner or later, retired people also come face-to-face with America's negative attitude toward senior citizens. Television, movies, books, and newspapers often make subtle fun of older people. They are often portrayed as laughable, pitiful, dull, or worn out. The effect of this message on retirees, who only a short time before felt competent and wise and capable of making important decisions, is that they begin to feel old and useless and unsure of themselves. Their self-esteem begins to decline.

At this point, many retirees begin the process of surrendering to the stereotype assigned to them by America's youth-oriented culture.

It is a process that is wrong and unfair! America's older citizens deserve better.

It is the purpose of this book to help older people regain their positive self-image and find meaning in their lives again. We want to transform the ending implied by retirement into an exciting new beginning; to help senior citizens find a reason to get up each morning; to inject the joy of living and a "reason to be" into their lives with more force and energy than ever before; to define and set new goals; and to empower their lives with purpose.

We want our book to be a pep talk — a short, matter-of-fact, heart-to-heart pep talk designed to be inspiring. We have been honest in stating the problems of retirement (no sugar-coating here) and equally straightforward in suggesting wonderful new ways to cope.

To other authors we leave the subjects of finances, investments, places to retire, Social Security, and writing wills. Instead, we offer meaning and purpose — a *lifestyle for retirement.*

CHAPTER I

A GIFT OF TIME

Carpe Diem! (Seize the day!)

It happens so suddenly: You are middle-aged and busy, feeling content and confident, a contributing member of society. Then, abruptly, you are one of the older generation. A senior citizen. Retired.

The reality of retirement can strike at unpredictable times and in different ways. It may be the arrival of your first social security check that startles you into the category of *senior citizen*. Or a form letter explaining your new status as *Medicare-eligible*. Maybe the realization hits you on the Monday morning after your retirement party. Or it may be a heart attack or health problem that propels you suddenly out of your job and into retirement.

It might be a small, tell-tale remark made by someone younger (perhaps a son or daughter!) who dismisses your opinion as outdated and irrelevant. Not too long ago, your advice was sought; your wisdom revered. Suddenly, your opinions are obsolete.

You feel the same but you're not the same.

How strange.
How frightening.
How shocking!

Of course, the physical signs have been coming for years. There are the wrinkles. They fan out about your eyes, around your mouth, and make peculiar patterns on your cheeks. Your hair is probably gray, dry, and thin. It stands up and out by itself and does what it wants to do. Your neck is no longer taut and firm. Your skin sags in peculiar ways on your body. Worst of all may be the aches and pains — the kind that nag and gnaw in the night, forcing you to crawl from your bed to gulp down two aspirin or fetch a heating pad. You remember watching Grandpa get up out of a chair and you could see that it hurt as he began to move, but you never dreamed that *you* would ever hurt that way. But lately, sometimes you are stiff when you first stand up, and it is hard to start moving. Just like Grandpa.

So what now? This is it. If your life were a book, this would be the beginning of the end, the last chapter. The whole idea is just plain depressing.

Or is it?

Well, you have a choice to make. Helen Keller once said, "Life is either a daring adventure — or nothing." You can negate life or you can affirm it. You can give up and give in; sit down and rock yourself into senility. Or you can rejoice because you are alive and can decide to "live, live, live," as Auntie Mame said. You can resolve to make *your* life a daring adventure and keep living until the last page — to make your last chapter the best one of all.

Take a few moments now to pause and reflect upon your life as though it were a book. If your life were divided into chapters, it would probably read something like this:

Chapter I: Birth and Childhood
Chapter II: School Days
Chapter III: Finding My Life's Work / Marriage
Chapter IV: Launching Myself / My Children
Chapter V: The Busy Middle Years

Now comes Chapter VI.

If you think of yourself as the central character of this book of yours, and if you were about to write Chapter VI, what would you write? This wonderful, blank chapter of your life is ready to be filled. Undoubtedly, you don't want it to be a sad, weepy ordeal. You don't have to be a pathetic victim. Instead, you can create a fabulous adventure, a marvelous climax, with *you* as the cheerful, active, enthusiastic, adventuresome hero or heroine! It does not matter if you failed miserably back in Chapter II, or if Chapter IV was dull as dishwater. You can still write a best-selling Chapter VI.

When you view your life as a book and yourself as its hero or heroine, you immediately rid yourself of the feeling that you are powerless. Many older people permit themselves to feel that life after retirement is a trap, that

3

only illness, accident, deterioration, and unhappiness lie ahead. But if you take it upon yourself to create your own wonderful Chapter VI, you automatically take charge.

You may want to devote your retirement years to something you've never done before, something you dreamed about long ago but put aside because it wasn't practical. Probably, throughout your life, you made decisions based on what you thought you ought to do, or what someone expected of you, or what you *had* to do to earn a living. Many of us spend our lives shackled by words like *should* and *must* and that paralyzing phrase, *"What will people think?"*

But now, if you look upon your life as a book, you realize that the time to be totally free has finally arrived. It no longer matters what people think. You have carved your little niche in life and you are in charge of yourself. Totally. You can create any ending you want.

Furthermore, you can be you without comparing yourself to anyone else. All of us spend time despairing over the things we can't do as well as others. We compare our homes and cars and clothes with those of others. We even compare our bodies and our assorted bulges with other people's bulges. Such comparisons are in the past. No more keeping up with the Joneses. It is time to let all your imperfections and idiosyncrasies flourish. You can be you. Happily.

Another happy thought: Now you can be good to yourself, guilt-free. You can do all the things you always thought were silly and self-indulgent.

You can savor and splurge and squeeze the living out

of life. You can get up at dawn to watch the sunrise or you can sleep until noon. You can lie in a hammock and watch the clouds float past, walk in the snow at midnight, watch the late-late movie without a qualm. It's time to wear your best jewelry, drink from your wedding-gift goblets, sleep under Grandma's prize quilt. It's time to fill your days with joy and meaning.

You may think you need to be wealthy to enjoy this sort of retirement. Not so. A successful retirement depends upon an attitude of becoming and changing and living and loving. It depends upon your understanding that retirement is a wonderful *gift* of time to examine your life, to put it all together, and to create the ending you want. It's a *grand finale* and a *new beginning* all wrapped up into one unique opportunity.

Plato said, "The unexamined life isn't worth living." Finally you have the time to sit back and examine your life, look at the dreams you had when you were younger, update those dreams and add to them to determine what you really want to do — and then *go for it*.

Want to write a book, learn a foreign language, or march for peace? Maybe you'd like to build a canoe, breed Saint Bernards, volunteer at a hospital, or coach a Little League team. Do you long to complete the stamp collection you began in fifth grade, take your grandson on a fishing trip, or learn ballroom dancing? Have you thought about continuing your education, studying computers, beginning a whole new career, or launching a new business? If there was something you never had the time for before retirement, now is the time to do it.

Retirement is for making dreams come true. Retirement is also a time to sum up and make sense of your life, to zero in on the important things. It is a time to gather up loose ends, remedy wrongs, look for long lost pals, hug the people you love.

Retirement is a phenomenal twentieth century concept. Throughout history, people worked until they died. Never before in the world has there been anything like the opportunity presented to you now. So forget all thoughts of a boring or pointless future. Truly, this chapter of your life can be a wonderful adventure.

CHAPTER 2

CREATE YOUR OWN NEW IMAGE

The image of getting older is changing…Suddenly age means style. It's in. It stands for vigor, class, wisdom — and consumer clout.
— Mary Finch Hoyt, USA WEEKEND

Once upon a time, retirement meant *old*. A person either worked until he died or until he was no longer able to work and then hobbled directly from work place to rocking chair. But times have changed and retirement has a whole new definition. Each new retiree needs and deserves a whole new image for his or her new lifestyle. It is an image consisting of three parts:

MIND, BODY, AND SPIRIT

Creating your new image is the ultimate do-it-yourself project. No one can do it for you. And it's truly fun and exciting to begin thinking about yourself in new ways.

YOUR MIND

Let's be honest. The vision of retirement that darkens most of our minds is downright depressing. It is the result of years of indoctrination via books, newspapers, magazines, and television. Our logic may tell us there are active, useful years ahead, but we continue to think of retirement as the beginning of the end. Words describing aging have been pounded into our psyches — words like *forgetful, hard-of-hearing, wrinkled, confused, sickly, frail, lonely, unhappy, dowdy, fearful, ignored, rejected, brooding, senile, and pitiful*. Visions of canes, walkers, wheelchairs, and nursing homes haunt us. We imagine feeble old folks trapped in squalid rooms, cold, shivering, tottering off to a senior center for a game of dominoes, or eating dog food because it is all they can afford.

This is a mental picture that undermines self-esteem. And it is so much a part of our lives that we hardly realize what it does to us. Gerontologists tell us that diminished self-esteem is the most serious problem facing us as we age — much more serious than poverty or loneliness or failing health. Since it is a fact that "as you see yourself in your thoughts, so you become," it makes sense to waste no time in changing our mental image of aging.

Make up your mind *today* never again to think of aging as a negative experience. Instead, think of it as simply another phase in a rich and wondrous life. In your life's book, consider it a chapter of fulfillment and joy.

Replace all those negative, self-defeating words with these wonderful, uplifting words describing older people:

- Intelligent
- Experienced
- Gentle
- Understanding
- Wise
- Alert
- Lovable
- Well-groomed
- Well-dressed
- Kind
- Calm
- At peace
- Happy
- Healthy
- Contented
- Involved
- Generous
- Giving
- Vigorous
- Interesting
- Informed
- Dignified
- Dignified
- Dignified

Repeat *dignified* several times because dignity has been taken away from older people by America's youth-oriented culture and we need to bring it back.

Make up your mind to become a role model for younger people and to take an active part in ending their false perceptions about aging and retirement. Futurists such as Ken Dychtwald, author of *The Age Wave*, tell us that as our baby-boomer children grow older (and it is already happening), attitudes about aging are changing for the better. Because there are so many baby-boomers, their clout is already being felt. They won't let the world put them down as they age. Take part in ensuring this process of changing attitudes. Be a role-model for the baby-boomers!

Refuse to play the "old age" role. Don't limit your life because of someone else's expectations. Reevaluate your clothes, your dresser drawers, your desk, your yard and garden, your car. Give away, throw away, or sell the things that drag you backward — the clutter and out-of-date remnants. Visualize yourself as a new kind of retired person — a pioneer in the new way of aging. Take charge of your thoughts. Several times a day, say to yourself: *I am a new kind of retired person, vital and alive. I am proud of my long life and many experiences. I am a very valuable person.*

YOUR BODY

Because it is impossible to live with joy and enthusiasm unless your body is in its best possible physical condition, it is necessary to focus attention on your body — to change your image of your body as it ages and to expect good health. A wise nurse once said, "One way or another, older people *must* care for their bodies. If they don't spend some time each day exercising, they'll spend that amount of time (or more) in a doctor's office — or a hospital."

Have you ever stopped to think about your body? It is truly a masterpiece. The ability of your body to preserve, protect, and rebuild itself is mind-boggling. No man-made machine could withstand the pounding your bones and muscles take, nor could a machine heal a broken part like your body heals a broken bone. When necessary, your heart can double its pumping rate. If you lose a kidney or a lung, your body keeps operating with the one remaining. Your body can function with only a part of your liver or pancreas or stomach or intestines. Your skin protects you from a daily battering by bacteria, and if you suffer a cut or a scratch, white blood cells rush to destroy the invading organisms. Because your skin is elastic, the damage caused by a fall or a blow is spread over a large area, thus reducing the impact.

So, even if you've developed some irritating ailments through the years, your body is prepared to help you heal and rejuvenate. Now that you have time to devote an hour each day to body maintenance, you'll observe immediate and amazing improvement.

Do you know that most ailments from which retirees suffer are the result of their lifestyles and that many of those problems are actually reversible? By changing their lives, people are often able to work miracles with high blood pressure, arthritis, coronary heart disease, diabetes, hip and knee problems, chronic bronchitis, urinary troubles, digestive disorders, and constipation.

Proof? A 70-year-old participant in Senior Olympics says:

> I used to be a typical couch potato. I'd hurry home from my desk job, sit down in front of the TV, and get up just in time to go to bed. My blood pressure

was high and my hip ached all night with arthritis. After I retired, my wife and I decided to try walking. My blood pressure went down, my hip stopped hurting, one thing led to another, and we joined Senior Olympics. Now we travel all over the country to Senior Olympic meets. We compete in race walking, horseshoes, high jump, shot put, discus, archery, and javelin. We love it. You have to see it to believe it — the way senior citizens enjoy Senior Olympics.

Or talk to retired people who walk every day and listen to their amazing stories:

Ten years ago, I had a heart attack and they thought I'd never make it. Now I walk three miles each morning and I feel better than I have ever felt in my life.

Arthritis hit me when I was in my fifties. I could barely move around the house because of the pain. But then I started water exercises and now I've progressed to walking every day. The pain is almost gone.

I used to take ten aspirin a day. For years. Now I watch my diet, I've lost twenty-two pounds, and I go weeks without an aspirin.

I was sluggish and depressed. I hated to get up in the morning until I started walking. Now I feel like a different person. Even my brain works better!

Of course, there are many forms of exercise from which to choose. Besides walking, you can swim, ride a stationary bicycle, or join an aerobic exercise class. There is some form of exercise for every body and every taste — just make the choice and get your body moving.

One exercise authority, Dr. Kenneth Cooper, has compared the human body's production of energy to a rocket booster burning fuel. The body burns oxygen, and energy is dependent upon the amount of oxygen that is delivered to the tissues. Exercise increases the body's ability to utilize oxygen and renew vitality. He advises us to go for a brisk walk if we feel exhausted and tired— *instead* of taking a nap! Try it. You'll be amazed.

The work of Dr. Dean Ornish is revolutionizing the treatment of heart problems. By changing the lifestyles of his patients to include fat-free diets, moderate aerobic exercise, and training in stress management, he is proving that heart disease can actually be reversed.

Give yourself every break when it comes to your body. Don't let false pride stand between you and the joy of living. We all know people who miss half of what's going on because they won't admit they need a hearing aid. Others fear walking alone because they feel unsteady, so they stay home. A cane for security could open up the world to them. If you need bifocals or trifocals, *get them*. Enjoy the wonderful variety of books and periodicals now in big print. Giving yourself these breaks is *not* a sign of senility; it is a sign of *mature wisdom*!

There are many other small ways to cope with some of the more common physical ailments experienced by older people. Think of them as positive steps you can take to maintain or restore the integrity of your body.

A simple exercise which might improve your life immeasurably is the perineal exercise. To cope with urinary leakage, hemorrhoids, constipation, and prostate enlargement, try this exercise:

Sit comfortably and inhale. As you exhale slowly, contract the muscles of the buttocks, squeezing and tightening. Hold; then inhale and relax. Repeat several times. At first, these movements may seem strange. If you can't feel the muscles responding, squeeze the seat muscles together and watch the pelvis rise slightly as the buttocks muscles firm. This exercise can be practiced anywhere. You can do it while sitting in your car at a stoplight, or while sitting in the bathtub. Results are often amazing.

There are even ways to cope with forgetfulness. If you notice that you're a bit forgetful, take a course in memory improvement and learn the many simple tricks and techniques for remembering faces, names, even ways to speed-read and remember. Exercise your mind with crossword puzzles, watch classes on television, play cards, or try trivia-type games. You know what they say: Use it or lose it.

When it comes to your food, take advantage of all the latest knowledge about healthful eating and eat the way you know you should. Most of us are beginning to learn more than we ever wanted to know about fiber, cholesterol, fats, and fish oils — but here are two ideas that seem sensible:

Do your grocery shopping around the store's edges. This is where the most healthful foods are kept. It is a matter of efficiency for the store: The foods which must be replenished frequently are often closest to the delivery doors. As a result, fresh fruits and vegetables; milk, eggs, yogurt, and cottage cheese; chicken, turkey, and fish; and fresh breads and pasta are around the edges of the store. Generally, as you move into the center aisles you will find the products with chemicals, preservatives, sugar, and salt. It is these boxes of man-made concoctions that clog arteries and manufacture body fat.

Why not give yourself a break and take a daily vitamin pill or two? Research indicates that the antioxidants (vitamins A, C, and E) are effective dietary supplements and we all need calcium and the other elements included in good-quality vitamin pills. Even doctors acknowledge the importance of vitamins for preventative health care.

One word of caution: We all know people who spend their lives maintaining their health. Their conversation revolves around their aches, pains, cholesterol count, pulse rate, and blood pressure. They carry little sacks of oat bran and vials of vitamin pills. They are so busy tending their bodies that there is no time left for living. Beware of this kind of obsessiveness in yourself.

Another aspect of good health worth investigating is relaxation. As an antidote to the stress which is inevitable in life, doctors now recognize the need for total relaxation to maintain physical health. Have you ever learned how to relax? You may think it is a foolish question, but many people live their lives without ever experiencing true relaxation. It is a skill that takes coaching and practice.

There are many places to go to learn relaxation techniques. Classes in relaxation are now offered by many hospitals and pain clinics across the country. Many doctors incorporate relaxation into biofeedback training; it is also offered at many YWCAs and YMCAs and is also a part of all hatha yoga classes.

Try this typical *relaxation script*. If you can't find a nearby class, tape your own voice reading it. You can then listen to it regularly, following the directions and enjoying the benefits. It should be read softly and slowly. Lie on your back, preferably on a mat or rug on the floor and follow the script:

- This is your time. There is nowhere you need to go and nothing you need to do. These next minutes will be devoted to your well-being. Be aware that the day's events and problems will wait as you settle into a comfortable position of rest, and retreat into your inner self. Bring your mind to this space which your body is occupying. Do not allow the frenzied experiences of your day to intrude as you retreat into the stillness.

- Now close your eyes and breathe deeply as you would in a heavy sleep. With each breath, direct your thoughts to your muscles. Allow nothing to distract or disturb you.

- Make a rigid fist with your right hand. Then press the forearm downward toward the floor. Press the arm toward your body, squeezing tightly. Hold. Now release with a sigh. Take a moment to observe that arm and hand. Compare. Now shift your attention to your left hand. Make a fist. Now press the forearm toward the floor, press in toward your body, squeezing tightly. Press harder — harder — now release with a sigh.

- Purse your lips into an O. Now spread your lips as you open your mouth widely. Yawn and then let your jaw relax.

- Take a deep breath and let it go. Raise your forehead as though you are surprised. Hold. Now furrow your brow as though you are worried. Hold. Now release with a deep exhalation. Relax your forehead. Observe how warm and heavy your facial muscles feel. Enjoy the sensation.

- Inhale deeply and bring your shoulders up toward your ears. Hold tightly. Keep holding. Now release and exhale. Observe. Rearrange your shoulders in a comfortable position and let them sink into the floor. Feel the heavy warm sensation of relaxation spread through your upper body. With each new breath, you are more relaxed, more at rest, more peaceful.

- Now tense your right leg. Hold. Tighter. Release.

- Tense your left leg. Hold. Tighter. Now release. Enjoy the feeling of relaxation in your legs.

- Surrender your entire body to feelings of refreshing relaxation. Feel each breath flood your body with tranquility, washing away all tension. Saturate your lungs with sparkling, healthful energy. With each breath, experience a deeper feeling of letting go.

- Thoughts have power. Visualize yourself as strong and straight; healthy and smiling; dignified and at peace. You are ageless. Content. Accomplished. Living. Enjoying. Each day is an opportunity. An adventure. A miracle of living.

- Enjoy this experience of total relaxation. Remember this place of peace and strength within you.

- Now open your eyes, stretch, smile, sit up slowly. Keep this pleasant feeling with you throughout your day. Use this feeling as the basis for comparison whenever you begin to feel uptight and tense.

YOUR SPIRIT

Until we retire, many of us have never had time to reflect upon our own individual spirit — that light within —the quality of which is uniquely our own and which, if discovered, leads the way to true happiness.

The search for spirit is an individual pursuit. Finding self-awareness leads to self-expression and, ultimately, to self-realization. Many faiths believe that it is impossible to experience true happiness until one has discovered the unique gifts, talents, and purposes that are his or hers alone. Wise men throughout history have advised that we trust and follow our own inner spirits:

Jesus said, "The Kingdom of Heaven is within."

Goethe wrote, "Just trust yourself. Then you will know how to live."

The transcendentalists believed in the individual's spirit as the ultimate source. "God enters by a private door into every individual…We are wiser than we know," observed Ralph Waldo Emerson.

Bernie Siegel, M.D., author of *Peace, Love, and Healing: Bodymind Communication and the Path to Self-Healing*, believes we are each given an assignment in life to discover the ways in which we are exceptional, and then to live a joyful life as we fulfill our mission. Each of us, he says, is as unique as our finger prints, but few of us live up to the potential of our uniqueness.

Find your sacred place, discover your special, unique gifts, and then "follow your bliss" advises Joseph Campbell. Following your passion puts you on a kind of inevitable track towards meeting people who can help you along your way; towards living the life you are meant to live. If you faithfully follow this course, you will be surprised at how opportunities begin to unfold and present themselves.

Prayer, solitude, meditation, and music are all tools that can be used in spiritual study. Or try long, contemplative walks. Remember that your quest is to find your own unique place in the universe — not someone else's place or someone else's idea of your place.

And don't let the "it's-too-late" feeling discourage your quest. It takes many years to develop the intelligence, creativity, wisdom, and compassion needed to recognize your own special gifts. Find your bliss and then proceed to let your gifts manifest themselves. It will be a wonderful adventure.

Creating a positive new holistic image for retirement — in mind, body, and spirit — is neither quick nor easy. It often involves retraining your thinking and changing your lifestyle. But as you observe positive changes taking place in yourself, you will experience reinforcement and a desire to continue. You will also observe that mind, body, and spirit are actually one unit. A positive-thinking mind is almost always found in a healthy body; pessimism rarely produces good works; and an individual's unique spirit makes his or her life memorable.

CHAPTER 3

CHOOSING YOUR GOALS

Most people spend more time planning a party, studying the newspaper, or making a Christmas list than they spend planning their lives.

— Denis Waitley, THE WINNER'S EDGE

Maybe you know exactly what you want to do now that you have retired. Perhaps you already have specific goals in mind, and you have just been waiting to begin as soon as your working days were over. If your goals are already clearly defined, this chapter is not for you.

But if your future is a bit fuzzy — if you have only vague thoughts about what you'd like to do and you don't know how to proceed — this chapter is vital. It is a hard and fast truth: *A successful retiree has goals that are defined and measurable because, no matter what anyone says about looking forward to "doing nothing," after a while those days with no reason to get up in the morning become dull, depressing, and seemingly out of control.*

As put forth in *The Winner's Edge*:

If your goal is to retire, you'd better think twice because true retirement is lying horizontally in a box with a lily in your hand. There have been recent studies conducted by the insurance industry concerning retired military officers and businessmen who are looking forward to retiring and just doing nothing after thirty years of hard work. Do you know that they live [only] six to seven years in retirement? Not much time to enjoy their pensions and just doing nothing!

Before you begin to define your goals, it is important to understand the adjustments involved in the transition between working and not working. You must cope with two big changes in your lifestyle. First is the loss of routine structure. If you have held a job for years, you will probably find yourself floundering without the familiar off-to-work-home-again format. If you have been a homemaker, your life has been structured by years of dutiful routines: breakfast-at-seven and dinner-at-six. Now, suddenly, the structure is gone and your time is totally flexible. Although this adjustment sounds easy, it isn't.

Second, you will face the absence of familiar goals. For years, you have been occupied with getting a raise, paying for Johnny's education, accumulating possessions, keeping up with the people next door. Suddenly, these needs are no longer pressing. The resultant change can be bewildering.

It is time to choose some new goals! A common

mistake many retirees make is not taking the time to think about goals. They dismiss the whole idea of goals as unimportant. They plan their budgets, study their investment and insurance programs, make elaborate plans for sickness and catastrophe, but never think about the wonderful possibilities for *fun* that lie ahead. Many of us have spent our working years making other people's goals happen. Now it is time to zero in on our own. Goals are what make retirement an exciting adventure — a great finale for your Life's Book; a finish with a flourish!

So, take your pen in hand and let's begin.

Start by making a list of the dreams you had when you were young. Think about the things you wanted to do when you were a child. Remember your teen years? What were your hopes, your daydreams? What were you especially good at in high school? What did you love to do? Write down everything. Include all your thoughts, even if they seem foolish and irrelevant.

Later, after you started working, did you ever say "If only I could quit my job and _____?" Or "I wish I could start over. I'd _____!"

When you go to the library or to a bookstore, which books attract you like a magnet?

Think about your accomplishments and your strengths; the things that, deep down, you know you are really good at.

Each of us has at least one special ability, one personal talent or interest we'd like to pursue in life; our *bliss*. Write down every thought that crosses your mind — every dream you ever dreamed.

The time is *now*. In fact, it is now or never so no more postponing or procrastinating. To stimulate your thinking, sit back and thoughtfully fill in the blanks in the following statements.

I would like to:

1. Study _____. (one specific subject)

2. Finish my education and eventually _____.

3. Travel to _____ (a specific place) by _____. (mode of transportation)

4. Learn a foreign language: _____.

5. Build a _____ or make a _____.

6. Begin a new career as a _____.

7. Take lessons in _____.

8. Give lessons in _____.

9. Finish _____ which I began years ago.

10. Take up the sport of _____.

11. Study my family genealogy.

12. Write the story of my life titled _____.

13. Write a book about _____.

14. Paint a picture of _____.

15. Take photographs of _____.

16. Work to further the cause of _____.

17. Help raise funds for _____.

18. Be a volunteer at _____.

19. Acquire and restore a _____.

20. Begin collecting _____.

21. Become computer literate.

Remember that you are never too old to do what you want to do. "I'm too old for that" or "I'd try that if I were ten years younger" or "What would my children think" or "I have to take care of a loved one. I have no choice" are thoughts that devour dreams, turn you into a victim, and deflate your self-esteem. Replace those words with "I can" and "I've decided to" and "Retirement finally gives me the chance to do what I want to do."

Open your mind and let your imagination soar. Anything is possible.

Don't hurry this goal-seeking process and don't skip over it. If it takes a week, a month, or even longer to define your goals, the time will be well spent. Understand that goals can be changed and redefined later. Each of us has an individual and unique path to follow; no one can find it for us.

One more thought about goals: Did you ever stop to think that goals are a cure for adversity? When things go wrong, when a sudden illness or a tragedy touches us, people with goals are better able to pick themselves up and go on with their lives. Individuals with purpose, despite tremendous set-backs, have been able to overcome them and continue the pursuit of their goals. (See Chapter VII.) Nietzsche wrote, "He who has a why to live can bear almost any how." It is not selfish or foolish to find a purpose and follow your goals. Think of them as a form of happiness insurance.

After you have determined your goals, it is important to write them down as well-defined statements which deal with the nitty-gritty details of your hopes and dreams.

EXAMPLES

You have always wanted to learn to speak French and to explore France. Your goal is "I want to learn French." Elaborated: "I want to take classes and learn conversational French so well that I will be able to understand and speak it when I visit France in five years."

You have always loved dogs and have dreamed of owning a show dog. Your goal, "I want to own a show dog," can be expanded to: "I will purchase a puppy of the quality to show. I will train the dog, study how to show him, and I will enter my dog in competition in the summer show of 19 — ."

If you have always wanted to learn to play the piano but you don't even have a piano, first write: "I'm going to learn to play the piano." Then, write: "I will locate and buy a second-hand piano, have it moved to my home, and begin taking piano lessons so that by next Christmas I will be able to play Christmas carols."

After you have defined and written down your goals, make several copies and put them in places where you won't forget or ignore them. One copy should go in your purse or wallet, one on your bathroom mirror, perhaps one on the refrigerator door. A determined, 75-year-old woman wrote her goals in large letters on a piece of paper which she taped to the television screen.

> That way, I thought twice before I took my goals down in order to watch television. It was a trick I played on myself, but if I hadn't done that, I wouldn't have worked on my family history. And I'm going to finish it this fall and give copies to all my children when we're together at Thanksgiving.

Now comes the last step in your goal-setting. It is time to make a *five-year plan* and to assign yourself specific deadlines in the steps toward accomplishing your specific goals. Miraculous achievements can be accomplished in a five-year chunk of time. Remember that five years will pass whether you are fulfilling your dreams or not, so you might as well use those years to your advantage. In five years, you will be so glad!

EXAMPLES OF FIVE-YEAR PLANS

- Goal: To learn to speak French and to visit France.
- Next week: Enroll in a French class. Begin putting aside $_____ each week in a special "Off to France" savings account. Buy a "Beginning French" tape and listen to it each day.

- In one year: Complete two semesters of French instruction. Gather material on touring France.
- In two years: Complete another full year of study and be able to speak and read the language.
- In three years: Begin corresponding with a French pen-pal. Take another course in advanced French.
- In four years: In French, write for information about all the places I want to visit in France. Keep studying. Make reservations for my trip to France.
- In five years: Go to France for one month. See everything I've always wanted to see and, while there, speak French fluently. *Hurrah!*

Goal-setting is exciting and fun! Making a five-year plan for yourself is truly an adventure.

- Goal: To make an heirloom quilt for each of my five grandchildren.
- Immediately: Go to library and check out books on quilts and quilt-making.
- In one month: Enroll in an adult-education quilt-making class. Join local quilt-makers guild. Study quilt patterns and decide on one to make.
- In two months: Determine the color scheme and buy the fabric.
- In three months: Complete cutting of fabric.
- In one year: Complete and give first quilt to oldest grandchild.
- In two years: Complete second quilt and give to next grandchild.

- Three-year goal: Complete third quilt for third grandchild.
- Four-year goal: Complete fourth quilt for fourth grandchild.
- Five-year goal: Give fifth quilt to fifth grandchild.

What a wonderful accomplishment!

- Goal: To become a freelance writer specializing in travel writing.
- Immediately: With the help of the librarian, check out several books written by successful travel writers. Read with an eye toward how they do their jobs.
- In one year: Complete a class in non-fiction writing at local vocational college. Continue to study travel magazines and books and to analyze how they are written. Buy *Writer's Market*, subscribe to a writer's magazine and study markets which buy travel articles.
- In two years: Outline and write five articles about local places which would interest travelers. Submit to magazines and sell, if possible.
- In three years: Begin writing about all places of interest in home state. Submit and sell, if possible. Try to become authority on home state.
- In four years: Plan and make a trip; then write an account of the trip for publication. Submit and sell.
- In five years: Continue to write travel articles. Attend workshop/conference for travel writers as a full-fledged participant!

Dreams *do* come true if you have a strategy to make it happen.

• Goal: To become a participant in the computer age.

• Immediately: List in writing how computers are used in the world around you. Talk with family and friends about their computer use. Find a teacher to help you and develop an "I am part of the computer world" attitude.

• In one year: Complete a beginner's class in personal computing. Learn the computer user's language (CD ROM, modems, FAX, lap top, desk top, etc.). Watch television programs on computers and clip articles pertaining to computers. Before this year ends, purchase your own computer.

• In two years: Complete a course in word processing and use your computer for personal correspondence and financial records.

• In three years: Explore all the applications of your personal computer. Complete the tutorials within your software package and begin using a computerized checkbook, maintain your tax records, inventory your home, and create a data base of records.

• In four years: Expand! Add a modem and an on-line package. Purchase and use CD ROM programs (encyclopedias, personal growth and travel programs, home shopping, etc.). Surf the Internet. Send E-mail to your grandchildren and meet friends around the world.

• In five years: Keep growing and enjoying the wonders of developing technologies. Use updates for your application packages. Continue your growth as a self-learner in the computer world.

If this sort of plan seems like an impossible dream, think again. Remember that you have full days to devote to your goals and that it is never too late to do the thing you want to do.

Each evening, before you go to sleep, think about your goals and plan the things you can do the next day that will be steps along the path toward making your dream a reality. In the morning, review your goals before your day starts. And if you need encouragement now and then, don't hesitate to use motivational tapes or books. They can be tools to help you over the inevitable slow spots.

Along the way, give yourself small rewards and recognitions. Take a friend out for dinner when you accomplish your one-year goal. Or buy yourself a little gift. You deserve it.

Someone very wise once said, "A goal is a dream with a deadline." A dream can last a lifetime and then fade away, unfulfilled and forgotten. But with a deadline attached, the dream will become a reality and the dreamer will experience true joy. For there is no joy like the joy of seeing a dream become reality.

See the next page for your Personal Plan.

FIVE-YEAR TIMELINE

Personal Plan

My goal is:

Immediately:

In one year:

In two years:

In three years:

In four years:

In five years:

CHAPTER 4

THE MYSTERY OF DISAPPEARING TIME

Lost time is never found. — Benjamin Franklin

Who would ever expect a retired person to have a problem with time management? After all, retirement means lots of time to do the things you have wanted to do all your life but had to postpone because you were too busy.

However, now you must face the frightening fact that all those wonderful things you had planned to do simply aren't happening. Time is literally disappearing.

"I'm busier now than when I was working, but I'm not accomplishing anything," is how you might put it. Or "I don't know how I ever found time to go to work — I'm so busy at home all day — doing nothing."

Thoreau put it another way: "It's not enough to be busy. The question is: What are we busy about?"

Many of us replace *business* with *busyness* and end up bewildered.

After you retire, life is suddenly full of sneaky, time-consuming traps. You turn on the television to watch the morning news and, before you know it, you've watched TV all morning. Or, because there seems to be lots of time, you make lots of little trips doing lots of little errands. If your adult children live nearby, refusing to sit with your grandchildren if you are needed seems impossible. And now that you have lots of free time to think, you devote the extra hours to worrying! You mull over your cholesterol level, the price of groceries, the state of the economy, the international situation, and your children's problems.

What can be done about disappearing time?

First, you must determine the important things you want to do. If you have done the exercises in Chapter III, you have already established your goals and plans to accomplish them. You have written them down and copies are situated in prominent places where you see them often. You have a five-year timeline.

Next, you must take charge of your time. The objective is to stay in control so that what you accomplish each day is by choice, not by *chance*. Organizing your time in order to accomplish your goals takes self-discipline and determination, but there are many tricks and methods to help you manage your time.

To help you cope with disappearing time, here are twenty tips compiled from a variety of time-management sources (see Suggested Reading List).

1. Begin each morning by planning your day. Make a list of all the things you want to do. Then divide tasks into *urgent* and *important*. Do the important tasks first. Many of us do all the little urgent things first (wash the car, weed the garden, sweep the porch) and never have time or energy left for the important things (working on goals).

2. Tackle the hard things first. It is only human to want to duck difficult jobs but, while you are fresh and the day is young, grapple with the tough jobs. The hours between 8 and 11 a.m. are the most productive for most people. Psychologically, if you have accomplished something difficult early in the morning, the rest of the day seems like a snap.

3. Finish one thing at a time. Instead of having many half-finished projects going all at once, complete one, then go on to the next. One completed task gives you the incentive to start another.

4. Designate one day each week as "errand day." Keep a list of the little errands you need to do (take clothes to the cleaners, go to the garden center, take your car through the car wash, buy stamps at the post office, etc.) and postpone all those little to-and-fro trips until "errand day." Then, organize your list according to the most efficient route. You will save time, gas, and frazzled nerves.

5. Always open your mail with a wastebasket, a calendar, and a file cabinet close at hand. Your calendar should have spaces large enough to write necessary

information. You will find that most of your mail can be thrown away, filed, or the information transferred to your calendar. By handling each piece of mail only once, you will save both time and effort. Bills should be filed, then all paid once a month in one sitting. On the same day, balance your checkbook and tend to all bookkeeping.

6. Keep a personal directory near your phone with phone numbers of friends and businesses you call often. Looking up numbers in the phone book again and again wastes time.

7. Do your grocery shopping early in the morning. Instead of picked-over produce, your fruits and vegetables will be fresh. You won't waste time standing in lines at the check-out counter. (Do you know that, for some reason, Tuesday mornings are the least crowded time in most grocery stores?)

8. Plan television watching a week ahead. Each weekend, go through the TV schedule for the week ahead and circle the programs you want to watch. Then turn on the television only for those chosen programs. When you are home all day, it is amazing how you can flick on the TV for a minute and hours pass.

9. Learn to say *no*. When you are asked to join or help or volunteer, say *no* loud and clear if you do not want to get involved. Do not say "maybe" or "I'll think about it." Many newly-retired people, afraid they won't have enough to do, say "yes" too often and

find themselves with so many commitments, they have no time left for their own projects.

10. Save hours of kitchen time by cooking double or triple amounts. Serve one batch for dinner, then freeze the rest in meal-size containers for use on busy days.

11. Control your telephone and use it wisely. After we retire, many of us seem to forget how to end a conversation. It is easy to babble on and on, saying nothing of importance. Think ahead: Have several tactful excuses in mind so you won't be trapped. One woman who found herself wasting hours chatting on the phone keeps a portable kitchen timer by the phone. When the phone rings, she sets it for five minutes and when it rings, she says, "Oh, there's my kitchen timer. I have to go." A very clever way to handle an awkward situation. Another little trick to use to control chat-time: Always stand up while talking on the phone. Your conversations will be shorter if you are not sitting down. Finally, "Let your fingers do the walking" when it comes to shopping.

12. Eliminate clutter. It is tempting to keep newspapers, magazines, letters, and clippings, thinking you will read or reread them someday in the future. It is also tempting to save empty boxes, wrapping paper, pretty bows, and clothes you haven't worn for years. The accumulation must be moved and sorted and dusted and accommodated — all of which takes time. Give

unused possessions to charity, and make lavish use of your wastebasket and garbage can.

13. Put things away where they belong. It has been estimated that we spend 20 to 30 percent of our lives looking for misplaced possessions! It pays to be tidy.

14. Use the small bits of time most people waste in *waiting*. Added up, those ten or fifteen minutes become hours. If you carry a little notebook and pencil with you, you can use that time to make a shopping list, plan menus for the week, or plan a party. If your goal is to learn a foreign language, carry a foreign-phrase book with you and learn a few words while you wait. If you foresee a long wait in a doctor's office or at the airport, take along your pen and a few sheets of stationary. Instead of idly leafing through old magazines, write a letter or a thank you note you have been meaning to write.

15. Learn to do two things at once. Some people use this "double-timing" habitually. They mend, sew, paint, or ride an exercise bike while watching TV; read while riding on the bus; file their nails while talking on the phone; defrost the refrigerator while cooking a meal; wash hose while taking a shower; listen to books-on-tape while driving.

16. You must determine how much time you *want* to spend taking care of grandchildren. Remember, you raised your family; Babysitting is not a duty, it's a pleasure. Naturally, you want to spend time with

your grandchildren and it's important to include them in your life. But many grandparents secretly resent the fact that they are expected to put aside their own plans whenever a grandchild is ill or parents need a babysitter. Establish the fact that your time is valuable and make rules so your children know exactly how often you'll be available for babysitting. (See Chapter V.)

17. Refuse to indulge in time-consuming, negative emotions such as guilt, anger, regret, and worry. They can devour your days. We all know people who live with bitterness over forced retirements; who worry about what the future may bring; or who stew over their adult children's problems. Accept your retirement as a fact; wait to worry about problems that may develop tomorrow; and let your children handle their own problems (not easy, but important for *your* well-being.)

18. Before you go to sleep at night, remember to do a little visualizing. Think about your goals; visualize your completed projects; fantasize. Visualization will give you a head start in the achievement of your goals.

19. Do not procrastinate. Before retirement, procrastination took a particular form. You used to say, "I don't have enough time so I won't start." After retiring, you are apt to say, "I have plenty of time so I'll wait to start." Both are excuses to put off doing the things you really want to do, deep down.

20. Remember that self-interest isn't selfish. Now that you have retired, give yourself permission to put yourself first. Instead of organizing your time around the needs of everyone else, organize your time around your own needs and goals.

If you take charge of your time, all those wonderful things you planned will really happen and your life will be fun and exciting.

How to Cope with Grandparent Guilt

Even though today's grandmother loves her children and grandchildren and, when occasion demands, will do anything in the world for them, she refuses to follow the script for the typical grandmother and live at their beck and call.

— Dr. Dorothy Finkelhor, THE LIBERATED GRANDMOTHER

Confusion about a grandparent's role in the family of the 1990s can be a problem, especially for a grandmother. Imagine this: It is 6:30 on a beautiful spring morning. You and your husband have been looking forward to this day. With friends, you plan to drive to a nearby town for lunch at a quaint little restaurant you have heard about. Then you will take a leisurely drive home along a scenic road that should be beautiful with the spring flowers in bloom. Just as you prepare to get into the shower, the telephone rings. It is your married daughter who lives nearby. "Mother, we have a problem." Her voice sounds worried and definitely hurried. "Suzie has a fever and she can't go to school. I took two days off from work last week when Billy was sick and I just can't take any more time off. John has an important meeting today with a client. Do you suppose you or Dad could babysit? I know it is an imposition, but we are desperate."

What do you say?

Being a grandparent today is not easy. It has a way of splitting your personality into two opposing halves. Half of you believes in the traditional grandparent — the wonderful, dependable, always-there kind you probably enjoyed when you were little. The other half of you is living happily in the present, enjoying the freedom that is finally possible now that you have retired. You consider your grandchildren an unbelievable blessing, love them with all your heart, and in an emergency you'd do anything for them. But you have no desire to turn yourself into their on-call babysitter.

This situation is especially difficult for grandmothers who feel a gnawing sense of guilt if they don't fit the old-fashioned grandma mold: generous and loving, almost saintly, with no desires or goals of her own, willing to drop everything and be at her family's beck-and-call when anyone needs her.

If, of course, you want to be the old-fashioned kind of grandparent, a daughter's plea for babysitting poses no dilemma for you. You will cancel your plans and hurry to help. Many grandparents prefer to be with their grandchildren, no matter what else is going on and we all understand how they feel. If, deep down in your heart, that is what you *want* to do, situations of this sort are not a problem.

If, on the other hand, you do *not* want to spend this chapter of your life constantly caring for little ones, read on. The confusion about what a grandparent's role should be is a very real problem for many of today's retirees. The irritation they feel when adult children take their time for granted can grow into a seething resentment. Many grandparents suffer this resentment silently to avoid family dissension, but it is very real.

The first thing to do is to understand why you have those guilty feelings.

Our generation is the Family-First-No-Matter-What generation. With all our hearts, we believe in the sanctity of the flag, motherhood, apple pie, and, above all, *the family*. World War II and the Korean War left us grateful for each other and for life. Our little nuclear families were solid and contained. Men earned the money and made the important decisions; women cared for the home. As good mothers, most of us dismissed Betty Friedan's unsettling Feminine Mystique movement and, without complaint, spent years of our lives in dedicated service to our families: We got up for 2 a.m. feedings; changed diapers (real cloth ones); led the way to kindergarten; washed dirty clothes and ironed; scrubbed dirty elbows and knees; baked cookies almost daily; attended PTA meetings, recitals, and ballgames; led Scout and Camp Fire groups; scrimped and saved for educations; and celebrated each

child's accomplishments. It was the way we were sup-
posed to live and few of us ever rebelled. We lived by the
rules.

The years have passed and things have changed.
Everyone, young or old, enjoys more freedom and privi-
leges. We understand our adult children and we are happy
for the opportunities and choices they have in today's
world. We watch our daughters have their babies, stay at
home a few weeks to get acquainted, and then hurry off
to pursue their dreams and continue their careers, full
steam ahead. Young people are busy doing their own
thing; tending to their own personal needs.

The problem, of course, is that children also have
personal needs. They need someone to care for them —
to be there. When they come home from school, they
need someone to sit for a moment, to look at their
spelling paper, to hear about the race they won (or lost),
to share their joys and their disappointments. When they
are sick, they need hugging and chicken soup and someone to read them a story. We see those needs, and we feel
an ache in our hearts as we watch tiny grandchildren
toted off to daycare or to sitters who may care more about
their fee than the well-being of their young charges.

We suffer from those old feelings we used to feel
when we had our own children: Guilt overwhelms us; we
feel selfish and that our plans should be secondary. Pre-
dictably, we react to our daughter's plea: "Of course, I'll
take care of Suzie, dear." Then we hang up the phone and
wonder why we are so confused.

What we must realize is that times have changed for everyone and grandparents are as different now as are young families. Like our adult children, we are entitled to enjoy new opportunities and new freedom. We have the right to live our own lives. Even though we would do anything for our grandchildren when a true need arises, it is simply not fair for us to become their constant caretakers. It is essential that we retrain our brains. Each grandparent must determine his or her own role.

Here are some ideas for grandparents to consider. Read them and see what you think. You may want to adopt all of them as principles to live by; you may want to adopt only a few; or you may think they are ridiculous and self-serving. However you perceive them, they *are* a beginning in your personal search for a way to avoid Grandparent Guilt.

PRINCIPLES OF GRANDPARENTING

1. I deserve to enjoy my retirement years, guilt-free. Now that I have reached retirement age, the number of years I have left are a big question mark. I do not know what lies ahead. After years of working hard, these days are my reward and my due. There is absolutely no reason to feel guilty about living each day to the fullest and doing what I want to do.

2. I deserve respect — for my time, my lifestyle, my possessions, and my moral code. I want to live in dignity. I want my family to realize that I am not less valuable

because I am no longer young. My time is my own and should not be considered less important because I am not working. My values and moral code deserve to be respected. It is my privilege to live the way I choose and to be respected as a dignified, independent person.

3. I deserve to be relieved of my duties as the head of the family. *Over-the-River-and-Through-the-Woods-to-Grand-mother's-House-We-Go* is no longer viable today. I am happy to pass on the baton, delighted to step down as family leader and decision-maker. With my blessing, the younger generation is free to make decisions and handle the family's affairs as I did for many years.

   I will do my very best to refrain from giving advice unless I am asked. I do not want to meddle or try to control the lives of my children or grandchildren. I will *try* not to spoil or indulge my grandchildren.

4. In times of crisis, serious illness, or catastrophe, I will stand by my family and help in every way that I can. In turn, I know they will help me. Support, after all, is what families are all about.

5. Grandparents serve an invaluable function. As an older family member, I want to give my family a sense of heritage, tradition, and continuity that only my generation can provide. In this time of splintered families, when young people are divorced and remarried, and step-brothers, step-sisters, step-mothers, and step-fathers live with half-brothers and half-sisters, feelings of insecurity, confusion, jealousy, and rivalry can arise. Grandparents who remain constant and reasonably

available can provide their grandchildren with interesting tales of a parent's childhood and other family history. I want my grandchildren to experience the sense of a solid family background that only my generation can provide.

Coping with Grandparent Guilt is deciding for ourselves to accept and live by the rules we adopt. As each situation presents itself, we must not be indecisive and wimpy. We are not responsible for the well-being of the next generation. We did the very best we could in raising our children. Now, it is their privilege to raise their children in the best way they can.

CHAPTER 6

HOW TO COPE WITH FEAR

Accept... the fact that old age and death are natural and inevitable, that to fear them is futile, and that they can best be faced with a calm and quiet mind, by ignoring them and gallantly living a day at a time.

— Wilfred A. Peterson

By the time you reach retirement age, you have conquered all the fears that have worried and tormented you and you can now live serenely and worry-free. Right?

WRONG!

During the years just before and just after retirement, new and unexpected fears may begin to torment your psyche such as:

- Will I have enough money after I retire?
- Will I be bored and face long, endless days?
- What if inflation goes wild while my income remains fixed?

- What if I get sick and can't take care of myself?
- What if I get cancer, have a heart attack, need surgery, need a hip replacement, develop arthritis or diabetes or Alzheimer's disease?
- Can I survive emotionally if my spouse dies and I am left alone? Will I want to survive?
- Will I be lonely when I'm old?
- Will my children ignore me when I'm old?
- Will I become wrinkled and ugly and pathetic?
- Will I lose all my hair? Will people take advantage of me when I'm old?
- Will I be the victim of scams and dishonest schemes?
- Will I be robbed, beaten, maimed, murdered? Will I be able to stay in my own home or apartment?
- Will I end up in a nursing home, forgotten and vegetating?

These are new fears compared to all the fears you have dealt with before. But you now have one distinct advantage: You have coped with enough problems in your life to know that you can handle them. Remember when you were afraid you would lose your job? Or when you *did* lose your job? Remember the fear that clutched your heart when your children were sick? Or when your husband or wife was lying in the hospital? Remember how you felt while you waited for the biopsy results to tell you whether or not it was cancer? Or the X ray to tell you if the bone was broken? Think of all the frightening things you have experienced through the years. Now think about how you faced those fears and survived. You did, you know. You faced the problems life dished out with amazing courage and resilience — and you can do it again, even better than before.

Actually, most of the things you feared never came to pass. One statistic tells us that 87% of all the things people worry about never happen.

In *The Art of Living,* Wilfred Peterson wisely writes that we master fear "by accepting the fact that old age and death are natural and inevitable, that to fear them is futile, and that they can best be faced with a calm and quiet mind, by ignoring them and gallantly living a day at a time."

Let's do it! Let's control our fears and enjoy and cherish each day as a wondrous gift, with calm and quiet minds.

There are some specific things we can do to erase the fears that creep into our minds.

1. *Fears multiply and spread out like ripples in a pond. Try to protect yourself by stopping them before they start.* When you think about it, our fears often begin with the media. We turn on the television and hear about the terrible things that are happening in the world — the tragedies and the catastrophes. Often older people are pictured as pitiful, homeless, starving, abused. Newspapers describe scams which rob seniors of their life savings. We read details about inhumane conditons in nursing homes and see pictures of people sitting in wheelchairs, staring into space with vacant eyes.

   The cure: Limit your intake of bad news. You can be well-informed by hearing or watching one newscast and reading one paper each day. Use the media for your own education and information. Then, turn the page or turn it off.

Another way to avoid becoming fearful is to avoid pessimists. For example, an old acquaintance is hopelessly negative. Every time you are together, he or she describes in detail how the world's financial situation is deteriorating and how inflation is rampant. After spending an afternoon together, you find yourself feeling uneasy about your own finances.

The cure: Without being unkind, simply tell your friend you do not care to listen to such talk. If necessary, limit the time you spend together.

You can even avoid *things* which trigger fearful thoughts. For example, a photograph of your son on your living room table reminds you that he rarely comes to visit. This thought then triggers the fear that you will be lonely and ignored as you grow older.

The cure: Put the photograph away. You can still look at it when you want to, but meanwhile you will be protected from a recurring fear.

2. *Take charge of your life. Fear loves helplessness, so refuse to be a victim.* Make it clear to your family and friends that you know what you want and you intend to handle your own affairs. Say "I can…" and "I have decided…" and "I'm going to…" Speak your mind. Women are especially prone to let themselves be led, advised, and to not make waves. By accepting personal responsibility for your actions and attitudes, you will control what happens to you and many fears will disappear like magic.

3. *Believe in your own good health.* Each of our bodies has a powerful will to be well. Make up your mind to exercise regularly, eat properly, learn to relax, have periodic medical and dental check-ups; in short, take good care of your body. Have faith in your own body's good health. Decide to "think good health."

   The late Norman Cousins believed in good health. As the respected editor of the *Saturday Review,* he suddenly developed an incurable crippling disease. Cousins refused to give in. Instead, he fought back with Vitamin C and positive emotions — hope, laughter, faith, love, and the will to live — and won his fight. In his best-selling book, *Anatomy of an Illness,* Cousins described his experience. He devoted the rest of his life to teaching, researching, and writing on the subject of the bio-chemical link between emotions and physical health. He believed that we are becoming a nation of hypochondriacs and weaklings who are obsessed with all the things that can go wrong with our bodies and do not understand that our remarkable bodies are capable of healing most ills. When we feel a pain, we reach for a pill rather than try to understand our body's message. Cousins reminds us that "we must learn never to underestimate the capacity of the human mind and body to regenerate — even when the prospects seem most wretched."

4. *Eliminate the words* if only *from your life. Regret precedes many fears.* All of us would change many things if we could live our lives over, applying the wisdom we have

gained through the years. But regrets lead to fears. For example: "If only I'd saved more money while I was working," leads to "I would have more money now," which leads to "What will happen to me if I run out of money?" Or, "If only I hadn't smoked all those years," leads to "My health would be better now," which leads to "Maybe I will get emphysema or lung cancer." Forget the "if-onlys."

5. *Stop stewing and start doing.* It is very difficult to be depressed and active at the same time. When fear begs for attention get up, go out, and get busy. Go where children are playing, where your friends are engaged in some interesting activity, or where you can help someone in need.

6. *Realize that worry is one of life's greatest time-wasters and refuse to squander your valuable time on it.* Remember your goals? Remember all the wonderful things you want to do? Time spent worrying is time taken away from accomplishing positive goals. It is just plain foolhardy to waste precious time worrying.

7. *If you do find yourself dwelling upon a fear, there is a trick you can use called* thought stopping. Thought stopping is a method of stopping a thought immediately and replacing it with another. Since your mind can only think one thought at a time, it *always* works.

   Whenever you realize that your mind is concentrating upon a fear, immediately take these three steps:

1. Give the command, "STOP." It often helps to say it out loud.

2. Take a deep breath.

3. Picture a pleasant scene — a peaceful seashore, a grassy picnic spot, puffy white clouds in a blue sky.

It seems too simple to work, but it does — and it can become a useful tool in handling the habit of dwelling upon fears. Try it; you'll like it.

Our minds are our greatest assets. By controlling our fears, we can enjoy peace of mind and limitless joy during retirement.

CHAPTER 7

ROLE MODELS

We all need heroes... A hero provides us with a point of reference.
— Madeleine L'Engle, A CIRCLE OF QUIET

Sometimes, no matter how happy your retirement or how complete your adjustment, you may find yourself feeling useless and over-the-hill. Temporarily, you forget about all the wonderful older people who are living rewarding lives; still accomplishing, contributing, and enjoying each day. They are people who have barely gotten started at retirement age and who continue to "live, live, live" far past the age when society expects them to sit down and rock themselves into senility.

Whenever you begin to feel as though life's opportunities are over, find a role model to remind yourself that older brains remain capable of creating and that life *can*, and *should*, continue to be a wonderful adventure far into the future. We all know that children need role models with whom to identify; well, *every* age needs role models.

In *A Circle of Quiet,* Madeleine L'Engle writes, "We all need heroes, and we can learn from the child's acceptance of the fact that he needs someone beyond himself to look up to…I need a hero. A hero shows me what fallible man can do…A hero provides us with a point of reference."

When you need a quick dose of encouragement, here are a few role models to give you inspiration. All are our contemporaries; most are household names. We have read about them for years. They give us a *point of reference* for our lives.

LIZ CARPENTER

Born in 1920, Liz Carpenter began writing a book about her life and what she had learned from living it on her 65th birthday — a gift to her children and grandchildren and any of the rest of us who are interested. She mailed it off to the publishers at age sixty-six, exactly one year from the day she started. The title: *Getting Better All the Time.*

You may remember Liz Carpenter as the White House press secretary for President and Mrs. Johnson. Her Texas accent matched those of the Johnsons. A plump, smiling, white-haired lady, Liz Carpenter seemed ageless. But when she retired, she found herself widowed and wondering what, if anything, lay ahead. She moved back to her hometown in Texas and began to construct a new life for herself. It was at that low point in her life that she wrote an article for the *Texas Monthly* about how it feels to grow old; about her dread of being put upon a shelf;

about her fears of not being needed. The article created such a response among older readers that it resulted in a contract for a book to be delivered in one year. Working on the book gave Liz Carpenter a whole new lease on life and a reason to hop out of bed each morning which she did — at 5:30 a.m.

The book offers insights we can all use. Liz Carpenter is honest and forthright about her feelings and fears, and they turn out to be the same feelings and fears we all have. Her wisdom includes the benefits derived from maintaining friendships and family ties. "How much better to be part of the network of aging friends." To discover new things. To care. To risk failure. To keep a sense of curiosity and a sense of humor which buffers life's inevitable problems. And to "accept the commitments of life by playing the roles life hands you, by suffering, by loving and by bearing life's indignities with dignity."

As for her children, she writes: "Yes, dear children of mine, I *am* spending your inheritance, but I worked for it and I want to enjoy it. The door's open. The beds are made. Come on down and sing along with Mom any time you can. There isn't anyone I'd rather have at my house than you. I would give up anything to have that happen — except my independence. So life goes on, and this old girl and this old world just keep on turning."

Recently, at age seventy, Liz took on the job of raising her brother's three teenagers. His marriage had broken up some years before and the children were living with him. When he became terminally ill, someone had to help and Liz accepted the challenge. The trauma of turning *her* home into *their* home and of surviving the resulting stress is told in her latest book, *Unplanned Parenthood*. Amusing to read, the book should be good therapy for many grandparents who find themselves raising their grandchildren.

Liz Carpenter is our kind of retired person.

JIMMY AND ROSALYNN CARTER

No one would have been surprised if ex-President Jimmy Carter and his First Lady Rosalynn had left Washington, headed home to Plains, Georgia, and retired to a quiet life free of controversy. Instead, both continue to be vital, active, caring people who live each day fully. We see pictures of them in hard hats and work boots helping with the physical work of building new homes for the needy. The organization to which they devote their hard work is Habitat for Humanity, a unique shared-work program which helps people help themselves. For ten years, the Carters have travelled across the United States to assist in this work.

Jimmy has also become an international mediator for peace. Despite some criticism, he believes there is a place for his work, and that he can act as a political mediator today in a way that he could not as president.

Having written nine prose books, Jimmy Carter recently surprised everyone by writing a book of poetry. Titled *Always a Reckoning and Other Poems*, the poems reveal much about Jimmy Carter's sensitivity, his feelings about his family, race relations, and life in Plains. (Only two other Presidents — Abraham Lincoln and John Quincy Adams — also wrote poetry.)

Meanwhile, Rosalynn too has been writing. With Susan Golant, she has coauthored a book titled *Helping Yourself Help Others: A Book for Caregivers*. It is a problem Rosalynn understands: When her father died in 1940 and her mother had to become the family wage earner, Rosalynn became the caregiver for her sister, two brothers, and an elderly grandfather. She estimates that there are 25 million at-home caregivers in the U.S. today. Her book is both sympathetic toward caregivers and full of practical advice.

The Carters are active, caring people who continue to give of themselves and enjoy each day.

JULIA CHILD

Now in her eighties, Julia Child is still writing and teaching about her favorite subject — *food.* She's a spunky, determined, down-to-earth role model who lives each day with enthusiasm.

Born in 1912 in California, Julia Child was one of three children, all over six feet tall. She laughingly tells how her mother used to say, "I've produced eighteen and one-half feet of children!" Julia was always a tomboy and loved to play basketball. She went to Smith College, graduated in 1934, and when World War II broke out, she decided she wanted to be a spy and joined the OSS. Instead, she found herself working as a file clerk, but her job took her from Washington D.C. to Ceylon where she met Paul

Child, an OSS mapmaker and diplomat. They were married in 1946.

Julia Child's fascination with cooking began when her husband was assigned to Paris. She learned to speak French *and* enrolled in the Cordon Bleu, became an expert in French cuisine, founded a cooking school with two French women, and wrote her first cookbook.

After her husband retired from the foreign service, they settled in Cambridge, Massachusetts. Her first television performance was on a review program promoting her book. She made an omelet and immediately people wanted her to teach cooking.

With all her heart, Julia Child believes that good eating is a vital part of good living and she is delighted that gastronomy is finally becoming an academic discipline in American universities. The first Master's in Culinary Arts degree is now offered at Boston University.

"What I like about my profession is that I will never have to retire," she says. "It's so important to stay as active as you can as you get older." She continues to write, give cooking demonstrations, make television appearances, go on book tours, and fit a lot of enthusiastic living into her daily life. Her definitive book, *The Way to Cook,* was published in 1989, and her latest television series of thirty-nine half-hour programs airs on PBS as "In Julia's Kitchen with Master Chefs," with an accompanying cookbook.

Summed up, her advice is: "Find something you're passionate about and keep tremendously interested in it."

CARMEN DELL'OREFICE

You see photographs of Carmen Dell'Orefice modeling beautiful clothing in all the finest fashion magazines.

Her face is elegant, her hair is silver gray, and her classical beauty is ageless. Although Carmen began her modeling career at age thirteen and, consequently, she knows *all* the tricks of being beautiful and glamorous, she believes that a woman can be glamorous at *any* age and that it is never too late.

In *Staying Beautiful,* Carmen writes, "Let me state unequivocally that it's never too late to start. Time is not a thief that robs you of your natural endowments. It is a gift enabling you to enhance them. The older woman's face is a piece of sculpture carved by time and experience. The color she applies must be muted and as delicately tinted as a watercolor. Any harshness only serves to emphasize the sculptural details she wants to soften."

Carmen also believes that every woman should find a style of her own. "Finding an individual style is one of the simplest things in the world. Go to a three-way mirror and have a good look. What are your assets? Those are the things your clothes must display and enhance. What are your liabilities? Those are the things to be concealed and played down."

Older women, she believes, have spent their lives giving love to others, pampering others, and following the rules set by society. Now, "you must begin to love and pamper yourself. You have earned the right to certain indulgences. You can give yourself permission to become the most important person in your life. Every day, in every way, you can become better and better."

"I don't believe youth is wasted on the young. As far as I'm concerned, the young are welcome to it. Those who have passed youth and go on longing for it seem to have forgotten what it was really like. I can't waste my time wishing I had it all to do over again. I would probably make the same mistakes, unless I also had the wisdom, experience, and sense of the ridiculous that it's taken all the years of my life to acquire."

A little tip she believes in: Each morning, she begins her day with a lemon cut in half. She drinks the juice of half of her lemon in a glass of warm water and rubs the other half on knuckles, elbows and knees to keep them light. And all day long, she drinks water — as much as she possibly can.

If you feel old and dowdy, remember Carmen's attitude toward aging.

PHYLLIS DILLER

Born in 1917, Phyllis Diller was a lonely only child in Lima, Ohio, who learned to be funny as a defense mechanism to counteract the self-consciousness that plagued her childhood. At age thirty-seven, she was married to college sweetheart Sherwood Anderson Diller, had five children and no money. Her friends thought she was hilarious so, encouraged by her husband, she decided to test her talent, and turned professional! Since 1955, she has been amusing us by poking fun at herself and laughing at her problems, including her mythical husband Fang. Her humor is down-to-earth, never off-color, and punctuated with her raucous laugh which has become her trademark.

Phyllis Diller credits a book, *The Magic of Believing* by Claude M. Bristol, with changing her life. At the time she first read it, she and her husband were locked into a constant struggle to keep their bills paid. The future looked bleak. The book seemed to be written expressly to fill her needs and for two years she carried it with her wherever she went, reading and studying it constantly.

"Believe in yourself," she says. "What magical words." After all, "life is a do-it-yourself kit."

In recent years, much of her humor has revolved around her fight against the aging, "drooping" process. She has had her neck, eyes, nose, cheeks, teeth and tummy "surgically enhanced" and she talks openly about each process. Her energy is boundless and her optimism is an inspiration. She refuses to let a negative thought enter her mind. She believes that bemoaning yesterday is counter-productive. She loves each new day.

HARRIET DOERR

The story of Harriet Doerr is an inspiration to everyone. She was born in 1910 in California, attended Smith College for a year, then married and became a busy wife and the mother of two children. In 1970, when she suddenly found herself widowed and alone, she decided to go back to college where she took a class in creative writing as a way of coping with her loneliness. At first she was afraid to let others see her work and was afraid to read it aloud in class. But she kept writing.

It took years to write her first book. Finally, at age seventy-four, she completed a novel and mustered the courage to send it to a publisher. The book, *Stones of Ibarra,* was accepted for publication — and won the American Book Award!

Harriet Doerr believes in the importance of exercising her intellectual energy by reading, writing, talking to people, and by thinking. To let this energy lie fallow is simply unacceptable in her view.

Doerr believes older writers have less energy, but a much longer view which is a great help. In *Contemporary Authors,* she makes this point: "I think fiction writing comes out of a mixture of experience, observation, and imagination, particularly imagination. If you've hung onto your memories, you're off to a good start."

Her second novel, *Consider This, Senora,* was published in 1994 when Doerr was eighty-three.

BETTY FRIEDAN

Thirty years ago, all of us felt the effect when Betty Friedan's book, *The Feminine Mystique,* was published. The controversial catalyst for the Feminist Movement, Betty Friedan changed women's expectations and their lives — and all of society in the process.

Now, at age seventy-two, Betty Friedan has produced *The Fountain of Age,* her latest effort to change the way we view aging. Feisty and determined, she recently spent a year at Harvard "immersed in a state-of-the-art study of aging" where she interviewed large numbers of happy seniors who have remained active and productive into their eighties and nineties. The result is a personal, authoritative, and thoughtful book.

Friedan believes that the denial of age and the attempt to cling to youth lead to mental and emotional stagnation. "Consciously affirm your own aging as a new period of development and you will continue to find ways to keep on developing."

Friedan has three children and eight grandchildren. She continues her busy schedule of writing, speaking, and teaching. In *The Fountain of Age,* she writes, "I began this quest with my own denial and fear of age. It ends with acceptance, affirmation, and celebration."

Betty Friedan nudges us to be proud of our age and gives us the courage to ignore society's negative view of aging.

LEE IACOCCA

Born in 1924 to Italian immigrant parents, Lee Iacocca grew up in Allentown, Pennsylvania, where his father ran a restaurant after losing his money in the Depression. Iacocca learned early how to cope with teasing about his ethnic background from schoolmates. And he learned early the value of having heroes. When he was growing up, he had two heroes: Leonardo da Vinci and Joe DiMaggio, two Italian boys who "made it."

While working for the Ford Motor Company, Iacocca gained fame in 1956 by introducing Ford's easy-payment plan, causing a fantastic increase in sales. He was also known for his involvement with the fabulously popular Ford Mustang. He eventually became president of the company.

In 1978, after his spectacular career at Ford, he was fired in a power play. It almost broke his spirit.

In his autobiography, Iacocca tells of his depression after his firing and about how he picked himself up, joined Chrysler Motors, and succeeded in the impossible task of turning a failing company into a successful and prosperous one. So what comes next for a man like Iacocca?

In *Talking Straight*, he writes:

> Over the years, I've watched a lot of guys grow old and turn into vegetables. You've got all these old turnips sitting around who were once running our largest companies. While they're still at the helm, they all say, 'Oh, it'll never happen to me.' But it does because they forget to plan ahead…I suppose I could load up the car and head for Florida where I could sit by the pool and play golf every day. But I'm not built that way. I have to work…so my plan is to spend time teaching and preaching.

He plans to teach at Lehigh University, his alma mater, where he hopes to pay back the college for all it did for him. "I'm going to try to be a cross between a savvy street-smart guy and an elder statesman."

Both of Iacocca's books, *Iacocca* and *Talking Straight,* are wonderful pep talks by a man who is the embodiment of the American dream.

JACK LALANNE

For as long as most of us can remember, Jack LaLanne has been a fitness guru. He explains that he first became interested in good health when he was a boy and his mother began to change her cooking methods, trying to make her family's meals healthier. His interest continued and he eventually opened his first conditioning studio in Oakland, California. Later, he became famous for his TV exercise class. "I want to get people off their seat and on their feet," he often said, laughing. He even married a sedentary, donut-loving secretary and convinced her to change her lifestyle. Elaine LaLanne became his TV partner and she is equally inspiring.

Jack LaLanne believes in the two qualities of pride and discipline. "If you've got those, you got it made. I try to maintain the same physical fitness I've had for fifty years. You'd be surprised what you can do." He believes that fitness in the years ahead will be less a matter of looking good, more a matter of extending life.

Now in his late-seventies, Jack LaLanne exercises two hours each day, writes books, creates fitness videos, lectures, conducts seminars, and travels thousands of miles each year.

He is still a frequent TV talk-show guest, always giving his upbeat message about healthy living. Remember that, "we are walking billboards for ourselves," he cautions. Our bodies and our postures tell much about us.

If you begin to feel as though you are too old to exercise or be productive, think about Jack LaLanne.

ANGELA LANSBURY

Of course, you have seen the program "Murder She Wrote" on TV. But have you read *Angela Lansbury's Positive Moves* or watched her video of the same name? In the process of demonstrating exercises and discussing her philosophy of fitness, Angela motivates mature women to remain mentally and physically fit.

Angela Lansbury was born in England in 1925, brought to America by her mother to escape the World War II bombings, and began working at age fourteen wrapping packages in a department store. She landed her first role in the movies at age seventeen as the maid in *Gaslight*. She's been working non-stop ever since.

Angela Lansbury uses and attributes much of her success to the practice of visualization. She believes strongly in the power of imagining oneself doing things: If you can *see* yourself doing something, you very often will be able to do it. She explains it as a form of positive thinking or daydreaming that can affect how others see you. Like an actor, if you see yourself as graceful or beautiful or dynamic, other people will respond to your cues. All the world's a stage and we're all actors, whether we get paid for it or not, declares Angela. She sees this technique as especially important for older women who reject the notion that only men get more attractive with age (an idea which Angela finds ridiculous). The technique of visualization is one which can help each of us become the sort of vital, active, retired person we *want* to be.

The suggested exercises in her video *Positive Moves* are sensible and her diet plan is wise. She is careful to stay within 2000 calories per day and eats a semi-vegetarian, highly-nutritious, and carefully-chosen variety of foods.

"Good health is more than just exercise," she explains. "It's really a point of view and a mental attitude. You can have the strongest body, but it's no good unless the person inside of you has strength and optimism."

JAMES MICHENER

Born in 1907, James Michener was forty before he decided to make writing his career. He won a Pulitzer Prize for his first book, *Tales of the South Pacific*, in 1947, and he has recently completed his 39th book, *Recessional*, at age eighty-seven!

Set in a fictional Florida retirement community, *Recessional* deals with the challenges facing a group of aging adults. Markedly different from his customary subjects, *Recessional* is a book which Michener felt needed to be written. Few authors deal with the subject of growing old, he explains, but this book faces the problems of aging head-on. Parts of *Recessional* parallel events in his own life, including the recent death of his wife and his move to a retirement community.

Michener travels, lectures, and teaches. He doesn't

anticipate slowing down for another ten or twelve years, and even then he knows he will find enough to do. He believes the most intriguing years of a person's life begin at age fifty, marked by fulfillment, additional bursts of energy, completion of projects, and time to sum up one's life. He advises all senior citizens to go find some excitement — it's good for your blood circulation!

STUDS TERKEL

Studs Terkel, a Pulitzer Prize-winning journalist, was born in 1912 in New York City but grew up in his beloved Chicago. He graduated from the University of Chicago in 1932 and from the Chicago Law School in 1934. He has acted in radio drama; been a disk jockey, and a sports commentator. Studs has written a number of books, among them, *Chicago*, which celebrates his home town, and *Working*, which celebrates people who work.

To people who live in or about Chicago, Studs Terkel is most loved for his popular, nationally-syndicated daily radio program. As the host, he is a master of the art of interviewing. Relaxed but animated, Studs has an insatiable appetite for learning about the lives of his guests, especially the noncelebrated. He gets excited by the discoveries of the poor, by the insights of the unrecognized. He notes that some interviewers never actually listen to what their guests have to say. They only pay attention to their lists of prepared questions. His approach is more intuitive; he listens to the pauses in a conversation and uses them to help him improvise during the interview.

Studs Terkel is angry about injustice and especially about the way older people are treated by our society. He is horrified by ageism in our society, and cites advertisers as culprits in promoting a kind of phoniness which he finds downright obscene. Studs appeals to our sense of vitality and our involvement in something greater than appearance alone.

Studs Terkel continues to create and to *live, live, live.*

PETER USTINOV

Born in 1921 in London, Peter Ustinov is an actor, a writer, a director, a producer, and an intellectual who speaks several languages. His life has been filled with numerous honors and accomplishments. Peter has no intention of slowing down because of his age. His public television series on the Vatican was first aired as he neared his seventy-fourth birthday.

In explaining why he has no regrets about his life, he says that he believes there is a reason behind everything that happens, and that there is always something positive to be gained from every experience. Peter believes that there is little point in wasting energy judging the past when there is much to be learned from failure:

> There is a tendency in men of my age, and in my profession, to pretend to be younger than they are. In Hollywood I recognize only half my acquaintances. The bald ones have neatly sewn hair; the hirsute ones have their ears covered in cozy

mobcaps of russet locks. And they all wear faded jeans with lumps of gold on chains around their necks. There are no old men anymore...Well, the young need old men. They need men who are not ashamed of age, not pathetic imitations of themselves.

His philosophy of life is one which can benefit all of us — no time wasted on regrets, get on with living, and let us all be proud of our age.

All of these people are inspiring, but if you need even more convincing that older people can be contributing members of society, here are a few more facts to consider:

- Ronald Reagan was a senior citizen before he was elected president.
- Pablo Picasso was still painting his masterpieces at age 90.
- George Bernard Shaw wrote *Farfetched Fables* at age 93.
- Mary Baker Eddy was still the head of the Christian Science Church at age 89.
- Arthur Rubinstein performed at Carnegie Hall at age 90.
- Golda Meir was a grandmother before she was prime minister of Israel.
- Michaelangelo painted his masterpieces on the ceiling of Saint Peter's Church between the ages of 71 and 89.
- Verdi wrote *Otello* when he was 74 and *Falstaff* when he was 80.

- Coco Chanel was still heading her fashion company at the age of 85.
- Grandma Moses was still busy painting at 100.
- Admiral William Byrd was the first person to fly over both the North and South Poles, after he retired.
- Justice Oliver Wendell Holmes undertook the study of Greek at age 92.
- Irving Berlin continued to write music in his 90s.
- Jessica Tandy won her Oscar for "Driving Miss Daisy" at age 81.
- W. Somerset Maugham wrote *Points of View* at age 84.
- George Burns said recently that he checks the obituary columns in the daily newspaper and if he doesn't see his name, he goes out and enjoys another marvelous twenty-four hours of life.

So find yourself a role model, buy his or her biography or autobiography and, whenever you begin to feel outdated, reach for it. It just makes sense to remind yourself that the joy of living is ageless.

CHAPTER 8

THOUGHTS TO GROW ON

No wise man ever wished to be younger. — Jonathon Swift

In researching the subject of retirement, a curious fact soon becomes evident: Young and middle-aged people who describe old age and retirement almost always bemoan the problems and difficulties, but when older, happily-retired people describe their lives, they talk about freedom and joy and contentment. They enumerate the many good things about being old. It is almost universal: The young dread growing old, but the elderly (if they have made the adjustment successfully) believe wholeheartedly that, despite a few inevitable physical limitations, the best time of life is old age. They know they are wiser, and life is far more interesting and rewarding than when they were young. They believe that they are better people living better quality, less-materialistic lives than when they were younger. (If only young people could realize this, their attitude toward growing old would change overnight!)

Examples abound. We could fill a book with them.

However, older people who love life and are enjoying retirement live by common rules which, though undefined and unspoken, become evident through observation and study. They are rules built upon the foundation discussed in earlier chapters. But, observed in daily life, they become four universal rules by which happy seniors play the game of life:

1. They monitor their thoughts and they are consciously *optimistic*. They admit this requires effort.

2. They permit themselves the *freedom to be* themselves. Compared to their younger years, their lives are uninhibited and spontaneous.

3. They *enjoy* each day and *live in the now*. No regrets about the past nor fear of the future.

4. They are involved in something which interests them. They have a *reason-to-be*.

OPTIMISM

It sounds so easy! Just keep smiling. Find the silver lining. Be happy. Look on the bright side. The glass is half-full (never half-empty).

It is not easy and it is especially difficult for older people in America. It takes a watchful eye to screen out the negative attitudes that can spoil the joy of retirement. We must be constantly vigilant and remind ourselves of our new, positive image of retirement. (See Chapter II).

Here is one woman's example of what can happen if you permit pessimism to enter your thoughts. It is a simple case of the old adage, *as a man thinketh, so is he*:

"One evening, my husband and I went to a lecture entitled 'Adjusting to Retirement.' The speaker was a young, highly intelligent professor of gerontology.

"He opened by telling us that he would examine what to expect after we retire and grow older. He would deal with facts, he said. No point in kidding ourselves.

"He began by presenting all the depressing economic facts about the aged in America. Then he zeroed in on the physical problems. After age sixty-five, he explained, muscle mass begins to diminish. The senses of taste and smell decline. Joints stiffen. Although the brain can function well, it operates more slowly. Everyone must expect hearing loss.

"Ending his depressing message, he said, 'Of course, it's not necessary to give in to a rocking-chair life. Inactivity and boredom are the main reasons so many people decline after retirement. But it takes a great effort to stay active. That's why so few people manage to do it.'

"As we stood to leave, I felt a pain in my back and the arthritis in my hip suddenly flared up. A siren screamed in the distance and I wondered if my ears would be able to hear something like that in a few more years. I was glad to hobble home.

"A few weeks later, I went to a lecture on 'Holistic

Health for Mature Citizens.' The speaker was a young doctor/radiologist — tall, lean, enthusiastic and smiling. He began. 'You are responsible for your own health and your own life, and you're never too old to improve. The body is absolutely amazing in its ability to repair itself. Age makes no difference. It is up to you. Exercise. Get your heart pumping. Move. Be active.'

"With his lecture, he presented slides. On the screen flashed a picture of a handsome white-haired gentleman wearing a bright blue warm-up suit. He was jogging along a country road. 'This is a seventy-four-year-old man,' the doctor said. 'He didn't begin jogging until he retired at sixty-five. Now he runs in marathons. He has turned his life around from being a sedentary, unfit, overweight, old man into a lean, physically-fit, ageless man who loves life.'

"He flicked to the next slide. 'This eighty-five-year-old woman is as limber as a teenager and she gets out of her house and goes for a brisk walk every day. She's fit because she works at it. She's vital and lively and interested in life — fun to be around.' I studied the trim, smiling, eighty-five-year-old woman on the screen. Her eyes twinkled and her cheeks were pink. I wondered if I could look like that at eighty-five. Maybe — if I exercised and...

"When the speech ended, I stood up straight and tall. Smiling and full of energy, I fairly bounded out of the auditorium. I had a new goal: to reach eighty-five like the woman on the slide. Life was an exciting adventure and I was in the bloom of good health.

"It wasn't until the next morning that I realized both speakers had said the same thing — that all of us can do

80

a lot to control the aging process. But there was a subtler message too: As a man thinketh, so is he. It was very clear that I had better watch carefully what I heareth! I had let myself be influenced by two attitudes toward aging. One had helped me and one had hurt me. I couldn't believe I'd been so vulnerable to negative thinking!"

This is an excellent example of precisely what successful retirees do not permit to happen.

With practice, it is possible to manipulate our minds out of life-is-a-trap pessimism into life-is-an-adventure optimism.

Here are twelve tips suggested by a group of senior citizens. All agreed that quick action is important. When we sense pessimism intruding into our thoughts, we must spring into action. Each suggestion represents a tested method to turn pessimism into optimism; proof that successful retirees are consciously optimistic — *they work at it*:

1. Go to the library and take home an armload of assorted books: a novel, a mystery story, a biography, and several "How-to" books. One of the books is sure to inspire or interest you.

2. Hurry out and buy a gift for yourself — nothing budget-threatening, but something you'd never buy under ordinary circumstances. Suggestions: an exotic new plant, a goldfish in a little bowl, a golf lesson with the best pro in town, a massage.

3. Write a thank-you note, but not a run-of-the-mill one. Think of someone who has been unusually kind

or helpful and write to that person's employer. For example, if a check-out clerk is always friendly and cheerful, write to the store manager about his or her fine employee.

4. Start exercising immediately. The type of exercise doesn't matter. Some people prefer weight lifting, some like slow yoga stretching, some go for a walk. However all agree that you must not delay. Start moving!

5. Put $5.00 in your wallet and make the rounds of garage sales. The challenge is to see how many useful, good-quality purchases you can make without spending more. (The lady who offered this idea said you will be amazed.)

6. Start something you've been procrastinating about. Just one small step toward its completion will be a giant leap for your morale.

7. Go to a travel agency and get brochures of exciting places you'd like to visit. Then begin planning a trip to one of them. (Something about this starts the wheels rolling — literally — and people say the trip often materializes as if by magic.)

8. Sit down and write a list of ten things for which you are thankful. Then, thoughtfully, recopy your list ten times. By the time you're through, you'll actually be ashamed to feel depressed.

9. Reread one of the books you loved as a child. Suggestions: *Little Women, Black Beauty, Heidi, Tom Swift.* Something about the wholesomeness of such a book restores the soul.

10. Become computer literate. You have the time to "surf the Internet"; adventures in creativity and learning await your retrieval. You will meet many new friends around the world, chatting on your personal computer.

11. Don't wait for friends or family to write, phone, or visit. Send cards, photos, videos, letters, and E-mail full of joy and encouragement!

    And last — the one technique which received unanimous and amused endorsement:

12. Rearrange the furniture. The combination of the physical work plus the change in hum-drum surroundings never fails to turn gloom into gladness.

One added suggestion: Buy a little notebook and begin a diary of "Life's Joys." This self-help trick appeared in an article by self-made millionaire Mortimer Levitt in *Parade Magazine*. Jot down the events and happenings that are joyful and memorable as they happen. Too many of us, as we get older, forget the events which have enriched our lives. A little book of documented joys can be reread whenever we need a reminder.

FREE TO BE

The second rule by which happily retired people live is that they permit themselves to be themselves. Happily retired people are not robots or victims; they are *individuals* who enjoy their *individuality*. They adopt an I-deserve-to-be-me philosophy and enjoy a self-confidence that allows them to act without first weighing all the consequences. It is a special form of self-esteem because it results in a happy abandon and spontaneity. The anxiety of being unsure of oneself is gone. Connie Goldman discovered this in her study of Late Bloomers:

> Late Bloomers have a strong sense of their own identities. Safely past the uncertainties of youth, they can enjoy being their own true selves and fulfill their own personal agendas: 'I am what I am going to be.'

Einstein said it in a different way: "The true value of a human being is determined primarily by the measure and sense in which he has obtained liberation from self." A happy retiree is definitely liberated from self.

To enjoy retirement, we need to enjoy our freedom. We have been solid citizens all our lives and we have done what was expected of us. Now the shackles of living a life of conformity, of being what society and family and employers expected, are loosened and we are able to enjoy a self-acceptance which we have never before experienced.

May Sarton describes it in her book, *At Seventy*. "This is the best time of my life. I love being old…I am more myself than I have ever been. There is less conflict. I am happier, more balanced and…better able to use my powers. I am surer of what my life is all about, have less self-doubt to conquer…" When we accept and live with this attitude, life takes on a joy which we could never have comprehended when we were young. "Trust yourself," wrote Ralph Waldo Emerson. We have heard those words over and over but they seemed impractical. To be successful retirees, we must live by those words. We must enjoy a let-yourself-go, stop-and-smell-the-roses, life-is-a-banquet, don't-worry-about-what-your-children-will-think attitude. Experiences which we once considered risky and frightening become exciting opportunities. We no longer give a hoot about judging either ourselves or others. We trust ourselves and are free to be ourselves.

ENJOY, ENJOY!

The third rule: *Enjoy, enjoy; live in the now* evolves from *free to be.*

There's a philosophical acceptance that comes with age which makes it possible to enjoy life more than in youth. Like Goethe's *Faust,* people finally accept their limitations and then proceed to find joy in everyday tasks and everyday happenings. Because of uncertainty about the amount of time which lies ahead (one year, ten years, twenty years?), the human brain adjusts and begins thinking in terms of one day at a time — and therein lies the ability to live "in the now." Wise men and philosophers through the ages have told us this is the secret to happiness — to live each moment and each day fully, without regretting yesterday or worrying about tomorrow.

We suspect that young people, through no fault of their own, are unable to live in the now, no matter how they try. There is *always* something to regret (Why didn't I finish college? If only I'd been watching Johnny, he wouldn't have broken his leg. Why didn't we buy that house before the price doubled?), or something to worry about (What if I lose my job? Who will take care of the children if the airplane crashes? Will the car break down before we can buy another?). Older people are able to live without this mindset because these sorts of concerns no longer apply to us. Grateful for each day, we are able to truly live. Life is transformed into a new and different sort of adventure. We are able to give and receive with no strings attached. We can set new goals which seemed foolhardy at an earlier time. We are able to live, love, laugh, and, when necessary, cry all within twenty-four hour time-frames.

There is no doubt about it: When we live in the now, life is more fun. We savor life's little pleasures: a long, leisurely walk, the sound of music, the smell of a pot of soup cooking on the stove. We love the beauty of a dandelion, the blue-and-white sky, the bright colors of the changing leaves in fall. A game of cards with an old pal or a cup of tea with a friend are special treats. We love our homes more. We even enjoy our solitude more.

There is an acceptance of the truth that problems go with the territory; that life will always contain things to be dealt with, but that the sun will come up tomorrow, no matter what peculiar and special problem is current. *This too will pass.*

A feeling evolves in the lives of happy retirees — the feeling that a wonderful adventure is unfolding if they sit back, accept what happens, and stop trying to change everyone and everything.

A REASON FOR LIVING

Last but not least is the *reason for living* rule or, as the French say, a *raison d'etre* — and it is perhaps the most important rule of all. Happy retirees invariably have a reason to get out of bed in the morning and they refuse to sit back and observe life; they participate.

On one of Connie Goldman's wonderfully inspiring Late Bloomer tapes, an enthusiastic retired woman says, "If you have something to do in the morning, it's actually a shot in the arm. If older people were given goals and objectives, half of our nursing homes could be emptied. They have to be given a reason for being. It is just like having, well, a blood transfusion. It's marvelous!"

Norman Cousins educated us about individuals who lived into their nineties despite serious health problems because of goals they wanted to accomplish; his own life was a testament to his words. He overcame two life-threatening ailments and continued to study and write far longer than doctors thought possible.

Of course, like everyone, happy retirees suffer setbacks and disappointments, even tragedies. Sometimes they pause in their pursuits in order to recover and regroup. But eventually, their reason for living grips them again and they continue.

We *must* find our own bliss — the thing we love to do, our own reason for living. It may take some searching and experimenting, but it is essential for a happy retirement. If you need to think more about this, go back to Chapter III and try again to define your goals. Let your mind soar.

GO FOR IT!

So — this is it. This is the conclusion, the summing up, of all we have been able to learn about being happily retired. One thing is certain: In the ways that truly matter, life improves with age. The cultures which revere their older citizens, honor them with scarlet-lined robes at age sixty, are correct in their regard: People *do* acquire wisdom and have more to offer as they age.

The negative stereotype of retirement is changing and people are beginning to realize that, when they retire, the best is yet to come. Retirement is the best time of life. It is truly a *new beginning* and a *grand finale* wrapped up in one wonderful opportunity.

It is our sincere hope that you, by using the ideas, suggestions, and observations gathered in this book, will be happily retired.

SUGGESTED READING LIST

A Circle of Quiet, Madeleine L'Engle (Harper Collins, 1984)

Age Wave, Ken Dychtwald (Bantam Books, 1990)

Always a Reckoning and Other Poems, Jimmy Carter (Times Books, 1994)

Anatomy of an Illness, Norman Cousins (Bantam Books, 1991)

Angela Lansbury's Positive Moves, Angela Lansbury (Delacorte Press, 1990)

At Seventy, A Journey, May Sarton (Norton, 1993)

Consider This, Senora, Harriet Doerr (Harcourt Brace, 1994)

Dear Me, Peter Ustinov (Little Brown Publishing, 1977)

Dr. Dean Ornish's Program for Reversing Heart Disease, Dr. Dean Ornish (Ballantine Books, 1990)

Getting Better All The Time, Liz Carpenter (A & M University Press, 1993)

Helping Yourself Help Others: A Book for Caregivers, Rosalynn Carter and Susan Golant (Times Books, 1994)

How to Get Control of Your Time and Your Life, Alan Lakein (NAL-Dutton, 1989)

Magic of Believing, Claude M. Bristol (Pocket Books, 1985)

Peace, Love and Healing: Bodymind Communication and the Path to Self-Healing, Dr. Bernie Siegel (Harper Collins, 1990)

Recessional, James Michener (Random House, 1994)

Staying Beautiful, Carmen Dell'Orefice and Alfred Lewis (Harper & Row, 1985)

Talking Straight, Lee Iacocca (Bantam Books, 1988)

The Art of Living, Wilfred Peterson (Galahad Books, 1993)

The Fountain of Age, Betty Friedan (Simon & Schuster, 1994)

The Way to Cook, Julia Child (Knopf, 1989)

Unplanned Parenthood, Liz Carpenter (Random House, 1994)

Working, Studs Terkel (Ballantine Books, 1985)

AUDIOTAPE:

Late Bloomer, Connie Goldman (For her catalog of books and audiotapes, write to: Connie Goldman Productions, 926 2nd Street, Suite 201, Santa Monica, CA 90403)

DR. DENIS WAITLEY is a national authority on high-level achievement. He is recognized worldwide for his studies and counseling of winners in every field from top executives to Superbowl and Olympic athletes; from astronauts to returning POWs. His audio program, *The Psychology of Winning*, has been listened to by more individuals than any other series on personal growth. He is the author of several *New York Times* bestselling books, including *Seeds of Greatness*, *Being the Best*, and his latest release, *Empires of the Mind*.

Dr. Waitley is a graduate of the U.S. Naval Academy at Annapolis and holds a doctorate degree in human behavior. He and his wife, Susan, are the parents of seven children and a "flock" of grandchildren.

EUDORA SLATER SEYFER is a long-time freelance writer and editor. She and her husband, George, are the parents of five sons and the grandparents of twelve grandchildren. Her articles have been published in *Mature Outlook*, *Vantage*, *Senior World*, *Mature Living*, *Country Living*, *House Beautiful*, *Country Home*, *Antique Review*, *Antiques and Collecting*, and *Lady's Circle*. During the 1970s she was a feature writer for Women's News Service. She is the co-author of *Gentle Yoga*, *MS*, *Stroke Damage*, and *In Wheelchairs*.